Baby Animals

A Baby Seal Story

by Martha E. H. Rustad

Consulting Editor: Gail Saunders-Smith, PhD

Consultant: Kathryn Ono, PhD
Marine Science Education and Research Center
University of New England, Biddeford, Maine

CAPSTONE PRESS
a capstone imprint

A female seal rests

on the pack ice.

Her newborn pup stays

close by. Its wet fur

looks yellow.

The pup's fur dries fluffy and white. The white coat hides the pup in the snow. Yawn. The tired pup falls asleep.

Bleat, bleat. Sniff, sniff.

The mother knows

her noisy pup's cry and smell.

Slurp! The pup drinks rich milk

from its mother's body.

Now the pup's mother is hungry.

She hasn't eaten for two weeks.

Away she slips to catch fish.

Good-bye!

Young seals stay together
on the ice. The fat pups can
barely move. A layer of blubber
keeps their bodies warm.

Time to molt! Raggedy, scraggly

tufts of white fur stick up.

The waterproof coat beneath

looks gray and spotted,

sleek and shiny.

Now the pup can learn
to swim. Its claws grip
the ice, and the seal slides
on its tummy to the water.

Slide on in! Hind flippers move
side to side through slushy
saltwater. Beat the water,
splash, and dive!
Now come up for a breath.

Look around. Hear those sounds?

Sharp eyes and keen ears find prey.

The seal's pointed teeth grip

slippery fish and crunchy crabs.

The pack ice is melting.

The ocean is calling.

In a few years,

the young seal will return

to find a mate and have a pup.

Glossary

blubber—a thick layer of fat under the skin of some animals; blubber keeps animals warm

flipper—a flat limb with bones on a sea animal; flippers help seals swim

keen—able to notice things easily

mate—a male or female partner of a pair of animals

molt—to shed a coat of fur, so new fur can grow in

pack ice—an area of large pieces of floating ice pushed together

prey—an animal that is hunted and eaten by another animal

sleek—smooth

Read More

Landau, Elaine. *Harp Seals: Animals of the Snow and Ice.* Berkeley Heights, N.J.: Enslow Publishers, 2010.

Martin-James, Kathleen. *Harp Seals.* Early Bird Nature Books. Minneapolis: Lerner Pub. Co., 2009.

Internet Sites

FactHound offers a safe, fun way to find Internet sites related to this book. All of the sites on FactHound have been researched by our staff.

Here's all you do:

Visit *www.facthound.com*

Type in this code: 9781429660624

Check out projects, games and lots more at
www.capstonekids.com

Pebble Plus is published by Capstone Press,
151 Good Counsel Drive, P.O. Box 669, Mankato, Minnesota 56002.
www.capstonepub.com

Books published by Capstone Press are manufactured with paper
containing at least 10 percent post-consumer waste.

Library of Congress Cataloging-in-Publication Data
Rustad, Martha E. H. (Martha Elizabeth Hillman), 1975–
A baby seal story / by Martha E. H. Rustad.
  p. cm.—(Pebble plus. Baby animals)
Includes bibliographical references and index.
ISBN 978-1-4296-6062-4 (library binding)
ISBN 978-1-4296-7096-8 (paperback)
1. Seals (Animals)—Infancy—Juvenile literature. I. Title. II. Series.
QL737.P64R87 2012
599.79'139—dc22   2010053929

Summary: Full-color photographs and simple text describe how seal pups grow up.

Editorial Credits
Erika L. Shores, editor; Ashlee Suker, designer; Svetlana Zhurkin, media researcher; Laura Manthe, production specialist

Photo Credits
Alamy/Dmitry Deshevykh, 19
Creatas, 1, 8–9
Getty Images/National Geographic/Brian J. Skerry, 13; Photolibrary/Doug Allan, 16–17
Minden Pictures/Gerard Lacz, 11; Tom Walmsley, 21
Photo Researchers/Dan Guravich, 15
Shutterstock/FloridaStock, 3, 4–5; Vladimir Melnik, cover, 7

The author dedicates this book to her son Markus Johan Rustad.

Note to Parents and Teachers

The Baby Animals series supports national science standards related to life science.
This book describes and illustrates seal pups. The images support early readers in
understanding the text. The repetition of words and phrases helps early readers learn
new words. This book also introduces early readers to subject-specific vocabulary words,
which are defined in the Glossary section. Early readers may need assistance to read
some words and to use the Table of Contents, Glossary, Read More, Internet Sites, and
Index sections of the book.

Printed in the United States of America in North Mankato, Minnesota.
032011   006110CGF11

Index

Word Count: 220
Grade: 1
Early-Intervention Level: 17